a season of
Grace

a season of

Grace

ELIZABETH M. HOEKSTRA

WITH THE WATERCOLORS OF MARLENE McLOUGHLIN

CROSSWAY BOOKS • WHEATON, ILLINOIS
A DIVISION OF GOOD NEWS PUBLISHERS

Cover and interior illustrations: Marlene McLoughlin

Book Design: Liita Forsyth

Hand-tooled leather for cover: Bob Roberts

First printing 2000

Printed in the United States of America

Library of Congress Cataloging-in-Publication Data

Hoekstra, Elizabeth M. 1962-
  A season of grace / Elizabeth M. Hoekstra.
    p.   cm. (All creation sings)
  ISBN 1-58134-207-1 (alk. paper)
  1. Meditations. 2. Autumn—Religious aspects—Christianity—Meditations.
I. Title.
BV4832.2.H595   2000
242—dc21   00-009049
                                    CIP

15	14	13	12	11	10	09	08	07	06	05	04	03	02	01	00
15	14	13	12	11	10	9	8	7	6	5	4	3	2	1	

Dedication

To my parents,
Tom and Cindy Marriner,
for teaching me to see things
the way they do.

The creation around us displays many parallels to the faith our Creator plants, tends, and harvests in those who belong to Him. The following meditations reflect on the fall season, a time of ripening faith, a time for storing up God's promises. On our small New Hampshire farm this is when my family gathers around our hearth for fellowship and cheer.

My prayer is that you will be encouraged by the life lessons we are constantly learning as the coming of autumn transforms our small world.

Come to Deeper Faith with Us

THE HEAVENS DECLARE the glory of God; the skies proclaim the work of his hands. Day after day they pour forth speech; night after night they display knowledge.

There is no speech or language where their voice is not heard. Their voice goes out into all the earth, their words to the ends of the world.

Psalm 19:1-4

The Lord Is Steadfast

Every good and perfect gift is from above,
coming down from the Father of the heavenly lights,
who does not change like shifting shadows.

JAMES 1:17

His Plan Stands

The works of his hands are faithful and just.

PSALM 111:7a

ALL THE EXPERTS predicted it. Certainly the dubious New Englanders agreed that no rain all summer meant no leaves with vibrant colors in the fall. The dire predictions raced across radio, TV, and newspaper reports. The lack of fall foliage colors would mean low tourism and reduced commerce—a far-reaching effect for New Hampshire and the other New England states depending on the revenue generated by fall foliage tours.

Of course, our God, who holds nature in His hand and scoffs at our interpretation of His workings, had a different plan. First, the swamp trees turned a deep orange, the colors reflected in shimmering pools below. Then the altitude trees, which started as a fleshy pink, blushed to a deep red. The birches deepened from pale yellow to sun-gold. That fall season proved to be one of the most colorful in years.

Aren't you relieved to know that the Lord is always faithful beyond *our* expectations? We expected no color; yet He gave us vibrancy. All of the scientific data pointed to correct predictions. But God still proved Himself above all of the exacting, most up-to-date information.

"God had planned something better for us" (Heb. 11:40). Aren't you glad to know that the Lord works beyond our limited expectations? Will you rest securely in these words of Isaiah? "My purpose will stand, and I will do all that I please.... What I have said, that I will bring about; what I have planned, that will I do" (46:10-11).

MORE SCRIPTURE FOR STUDY:
Psalm 33:9-15; Isaiah 14:24, 26-27;
1 Corinthians 1:9; 2 Timothy 2:13

Feeling Bare

All the trees of the field will clap their hands.

ISAIAH 55:12b

HAVE YOU EVER NOTICED that trees clap when they have no leaves? When branches are stripped bare by fall winds, they seem to scratch the sky. If their twig ends were inked, the stretched-canvas sky would be streaked with wide arcs and jagged lines—a mural of praise!

The wind clatters the branches against one another, making a soulful, low-pitched chorus. Are they clapping? Yes! They are making a joyful noise in the way they were created. Are they swaying in praise to the Lord? You bet! Aren't their branches all stretched heavenward?

I feel a lesson in the bare branches. Even when I'm stripped bare to a point of being vulnerable before the Lord, I can still praise Him. How about you? Like the trees, maybe we could be even louder in our praise when we feel exposed.

When our souls are exposed, we recognize our need for Him. Stripped down to our true selves with only our humanity as a covering, we recognize how much we need to be clothed in His righteousness. "May your priests be clothed with righteousness; may your saints sing for joy" (Ps. 132:9). We can even praise Him in advance, believing in faith that He'll bring about spiritual growth in our lives.

"Nothing in all creation is hidden from God's sight. Everything is uncovered and laid bare before the eyes of him to whom we must give account" (Heb. 4:13). Are you feeling especially exposed in an area of your life—maybe in a relationship, or in your work? Can you praise Him anyway with outstretched, clapping hands? Will you concentrate on praising Him this week, knowing that your bareness will be clothed with a veil of humility, a robe of security, or with shoes of grace?

MORE SCRIPTURE FOR STUDY:
Genesis 3:21; Psalm 45:13-15;
Matthew 6:28-34; Ephesians 6:10-18

Unhealthy Treasures

Where your treasure is, there your heart will be also.

MATTHEW 6:21

THEY CHATTER incessantly. I can even hear them through closed windows. They chase each other over rocks and the lawn. They climb trees and jump from branch to branch. And when they get mad, watch out! Screeching ensues.

My overactive kids, you think? No, the resident chipmunks.

Fall is their time for gathering acorns for winter. They store their cache in stone walls, tree trunks, and underground. They don't just have one or two storage haunts—they have multiple places just in case one gets raided or destroyed. But that doesn't mean they aren't protective of their winter food.

One day my son Jordan knocked loose a few rocks from one of the stone walls along our property edge. A small avalanche of black, rotten acorns rolled out. A chipmunk, unnoticed until then, screeched as if Jordan had stepped on his tail! I would say Jordan had discovered the chipmunk's treasure spot.

We all might have treasure spots that, if disturbed, we would screech about too. What do we hold dear that may be "off limits" to others? You know those places deep in your inner recesses that you haven't even allowed the Lord to touch. Is one an unhealthy attitude, selfish motivation, a miserly spirit, or a jealous nature? Why are we so afraid of these "treasures" being disturbed? Why do we guard them so rigorously? Because they are *ours*. Even if they are rotten and unhealthy, we hang on to them because we are uncertain about how to let go of them.

This week, ask the Lord to reveal to you what your unhealthy treasures may be. Ask Him to replace those treasures with the nuggets of holiness. "Flee the evil desires of youth, and pursue righteousness, faith, love and peace, along with those who call on the Lord out of a pure heart" (2 Tim. 2:22).

MORE SCRIPTURE FOR STUDY:
1 Chronicles 29:3; Proverbs 10:2;
Matthew 6:19-24; Hebrews 9:14

Living-Color Faith

*Let there be lights in the expanse of the sky to separate the day
from the night, and let them serve as signs to mark
seasons and days and years.*

GENESIS 1:14

THE TURNING OF SEASONS certainly reflects the passage of time in our
Christian journey. When we are new believers, we are like fresh spring and summer grass—full of enthusiasm and the desire to grow. Maturity comes in the fall
season of our faith. Just as the New England oak, maple, and birch leaves turn
eye-catching shades of deep orange, dark red, and golden yellow, we also take
on an array of colorful features as we mature in season.

Our uniqueness can be seen through the array of gifts God has given us.
As you've matured in your faith, have you noticed how the Lord helps you to
grow ever deeper in your giftedness? Maybe you started your faith walk with a
love of teaching. As you've matured, the Lord has grown that passion to include
ministering through speaking at retreats and conferences. In what ways has

the Lord brought your talents to fruition? Can you see how the maturity of your faith has spread beyond yourself to capture the eye of a broader audience?

The Lord is never content for us to remain at status quo in our gifts. His desire is to see us grow in our talents in order to edify others. How are we certain of this? "Being confident of this, that he who began a good work in you will carry it on to completion until the day of Christ Jesus" (Phil. 1:6). What's "completion?" Completion is the fall season of our faith, when our faith is in "living color."

A spectrum of colors will take over the New England landscape in the next few weeks. Will you thank the Lord for bringing you into the fall season of vibrancy in your faith, and trust Him to bring you into the full "colors" of your giftedness?

MORE SCRIPTURE FOR STUDY:
Psalm 138:8; Matthew 25:14-30;
1 Corinthians 7:7; James 1:4

Gifts of Splendor

The sun has one kind of splendor, the moon another and the stars
another; and star differs from star in splendor.

1 CORINTHIANS 15:41

WHEN I PICK BRANCHES of colored leaves to bring inside for decoration, I always look for a variety of colors, sizes, shapes, and types. I like the variety. Each New England leaf is different from those around it. Its shading may be deeper or less vivid than its neighbors. It may be flat or a little wrinkled along the edges. It may be a gigantic oak leaf or a young, tiny maple leaf. But are the leaves bothered by their differences? No.

This acceptance and appreciation of variety is another indicator of a maturing "fall faith." As we grow in our uniqueness we start to take on a less critical view of other people. Instead we find a growing tolerance for differences. We may find that we actually seek out others with gifts that differ from ours. We realize that we combine to create a sprinkling of varied colors, shapes, and sizes. As the above verse says, "star differs from star in splendor." But *all* are stars!

Isn't it the same for us? We differ immensely from each other; yet each of us can radiate God's love and light.

In the maturity of "fall faith" we can see one another's uniqueness and "splendor" without feeling threatened or critical. In what ways do we hold onto the young faith of a critical spirit? As you grow in your faith this fall, will you pray for opportunities to see differences in others as the "splendor" God created in each of us?

MORE SCRIPTURE FOR STUDY:
Proverbs 9:6, 9-12; Daniel 12:3;
Romans 10:11-13;
1 Corinthians 1:10; 12:25

Growing New Coats

You have taken off your old self with its practices and have put on
the new self, which is being renewed in knowledge
in the image of its Creator.

COLOSSIANS 3:9-10

FUR EVERYWHERE. That's how October always feels to me. Though October is one of my favorite months, it also brings out one of my biggest complaints on a farm: all of the animals shed during October. For our farm that means a house and barn full of floating hairs that tickle my nose, get caught in my throat, and stick to all of the furniture, my clothes, and even the cars. My kitchen broom stands ready at the counter to sweep five to six times a day.

What was God's purpose when He designed northern animals to shed before winter? To prepare them for winter by giving them a warmer coat to insulate them against colder temperatures and snow. Why? A fine summer coat won't keep a northern animal warm. So twice a year the animals shed: in the spring to get rid of their heavy winter coats, and in the fall to grow winter coats.

While paging through my Bible, I was reminded of the animal-shedding phenomenon when I read the above verse. We too have to shed our old selves—our past practices or attitudes—to encourage the new growth to come in. The new growth can't just grow over the old growth. The old must go first.

As you shed a layer of your old self, pray for the new growth God will provide in you. Like the animals, there is a purpose for the new growth. Maybe you require an extra layer of protecting love, humility, or patience. Will you thank Him now for providing you with His new protective growth?

MORE SCRIPTURE FOR STUDY:
Psalm 51:6-10; Ezekiel 11:18-20;
2 Corinthians 5:17; Ephesians 4:22-24

The Way Home

When you see the ark of the covenant ... follow it.
Then you will know which way to go,
since you have never been this way before.

JOSHUA 3:3-4a

HORSES ARE KNOWN for their homing instinct. Once, while riding my old mare, Foxfyre, she proved that instinct to me. Low branches, snagging bushes, and downed trees proved obstacles as I attempted to find a connection between two trails. I generally have a good sense of direction, but after navigating around logs, bushes, streams, and thickets, I realized that I was lost. I couldn't even turn around and retrace my steps. There were no tracks visible in the littered undergrowth.

I felt a twinge of panic. I halted my horse and looked at the sun, getting a vague idea of which way was home. I dropped the reins and said, "Go home, Foxfyre." She took my cue and unerringly picked her way to the nearest road. Although we were scratched and tired, we found our way easily from there.

The words from Joshua echoed in my mind: "You have never been this way before." It's scary to be in a place or situation where you have never been before. The terrain is unfamiliar and you don't know the dangerous spots.

Joshua had assurance from the Lord that although the land they were entering was new to them, He would faithfully lead them. Is it any different for us? Sometimes He may lead us into uncharted territory in our faith walks; yet He faithfully walks before us as our Guide. The Israelites followed the Lord's ark of the covenant just as we follow His written covenant to us in His Word.

I'm glad I don't need to know the way. I'm content to let God take the lead and bring me safely home.

MORE SCRIPTURE FOR STUDY:
Deuteronomy 26:16-19; Isaiah 55:8-9;
Jeremiah 6:16; John 10:3-5

Resting in Hope

We know that in all things God works for the good of those who love him, who have been called according to his purpose.

ROMANS 8:28

A FLASH OF SCARLET caught my eye as I walked the woodsy trail behind my home. Among the fading browns near the floor of the woods I found a single red seed pod on a solitary stalk. I recognized it as spring's painted trillium. In the fall, its white petals with their unique blaze of red were crumpled and dried. It looked dejected, with the one thought of hope showing red.

I later learned that the trillium reproduces in two ways: from its underground dormant bulb and from seeds in the red pod. It reminded me again of how nature's pattern so often mirrors our lives of faith. Our heavenly Father's economy allows the loss of something good and beautiful to make way, in time, for a better thing. When we experience loss or disappointment there are always new seeds for a refreshed life.

Loss comes in all forms, from the death of a loved friend or family member to the end of a long-held dream. Yet I'm convinced that in every difficult experience there is the promise of something good and beautiful to come if my heart surrenders and my hands let go of the hurt.

In the past I've carried hurts for years that I hadn't relinquished to the Lord. These included broken relationships, unforgiveness, and disappointment over a long-term situation. How can these possibly regenerate into something good and beautiful if I'm holding onto them too tightly? They can't. I've learned that I have a responsibility to lay my feelings of loss at the foot of the cross. God won't pry the feelings out of my hands until I'm ready to release them. It's my call.

God's seeds of abiding hope, goodness, and grace flashed in my mind when I saw that red seed pod. Are you also willing to rest in the hope of assured growth during the fall season of your faith even if you're in for a long wait until spring?

MORE SCRIPTURE FOR STUDY:
Psalm 86; Isaiah 40:28-31; 1 Peter 1:3-9;
Revelation 21:1-7

Attitude Places

Though we live in the world, we do not wage war as the world does....
We take captive every thought to make it obedient to Christ.

2 CORINTHIANS 10:3-5

THE WINDS OF OCTOBER strip the leaves from their branches and send them hurtling through the air until something halts them in their flight. They may skitter to a stop against a fence post, the foundation of a house, or the length of a stone wall. There the leaves congregate, as if they are communal hostages of the solid surface they are up against.

Is this scenario starting to sound familiar? Don't we too sometimes congregate where others are simply because they are there? I'm not talking about actual places. I'm talking more about the "attitude places:" the rocky crags of gossip, the cement wall of stubbornness, or the standing post of complaining. It's much easier to "go with the flow" and be part of a group than to be independent in thought and action.

What do we do with an accumulation of stray leaves? We rake them together, bag them, then burn or mulch them. The places that held the leaves hostage are now exposed. The leaves' moisture won't rot the fence post, their depth won't cover the pretty granite foundation, nor will they fill in the gaps in the stone walls.

Our inner environments can be similarly improved. As the above verse notes, we may live in the world but we don't have to be a part of the world. Leaves don't have a choice about the group in which they land. We do, however.

What groups have you landed in that have held you in an "attitude place"? Office gossip and complaining are typical parts of the water cooler network. Can you strike out in independence and remove yourself from such a place? Will you take "captive every thought" that contributes to an unhealthy group mentality?

MORE SCRIPTURE FOR STUDY:
Proverbs 11:2-3, 9-13; Isaiah 28:6;
Ephesians 4:29-5:2; James 1:26-27

Glory in Creation

And God said,
"Let the waters teem with living creatures,
and let birds fly above the earth
across the expanse of the sky."

GENESIS 1:20

I HEARD GEESE HONKING, coming up behind me low and loud. I stopped walking and turned to watch them. Even as I looked overhead they were right there, just above the trees. They were so close I could hear the whoosh from the downdraft of their flapping wings. I saw their round, silky underbellies and felt a hushed breeze after they passed. I wished I could have reached up to touch them, letting my fingertips trace their downy feathered bellies. But the group of ten were already gone, most likely having zeroed in on the pond about half a mile west of our home for their evening's rest.

I marveled at this brief moment. It felt like a gift. I had a momentary understanding of the driving force of their instinctual migration. "We need to get there, get there, get there" was the unvoiced refrain of each wing beat. I whispered after them, "Take me with you!"

At times like these I am amazed at the diversity of God's creation and the most intricate detail of the instincts He created. Birds hatch from eggs and instantly open their beaks to be fed. Wild, four-legged mammals stand, suckle, and are capable of running within an hour after birth. The queen African termite lives for twelve years underground, laying millions of eggs. She never sees daylight nor moves from her laying spot. Butterflies fly thousands of miles to their winter grounds.

Why did the Lord create nature with such complexity? Because He could. He could have made all of the animals to be about the same size and shape with similar habitat needs. But right from the start He created diversity. Why? Simply as a display of His glory. I'm impressed. Aren't you?

Revere His name with me: "Holy, holy, holy is the LORD Almighty; the whole earth is full of his glory" (Isa. 6:3).

MORE SCRIPTURE FOR STUDY:
Exodus 15:11; Job 39; Psalm 19:1-4;
Revelation 4:8-11

A God for All Seasons

*I am still confident of this: I will see the goodness of the LORD
in the land of the living.*

PSALM 27:13

DURING THE FALL the leaves change color, the air feels crisp, the lakes and streams settle in cold, and the fields begin to brown from frost. Despite what seems all around as a slowing of life and imminent death, I can echo David's words: "I am still confident of this: I will see the goodness of the LORD in the land of the living."

Just because a New England fall halts the growth of plant life, that doesn't mean God's goodness has stopped. The Lord created the seasons to remind us of our seasonal nature in spirit and body. But His feelings toward us are not seasonal. His love and forgiveness never diminish, never turn bitter, and never grow cold. Instead He is always nurturing our souls, increasing our faith, and offering protection.

How do we keep the confidence that David speaks of—the assured hope that we will always see God's goodness in His land? As Jeremiah wrote in

Lamentations, "Yet this I call to mind and therefore I have hope: Because of the LORD's great love we are not consumed, for his compassions never fail" (3:21-22). His love is not consumed, stripped, or dying like the fall leaves and grasses.

What does our confidence and hope produce? "Blessed is the man who trusts in the LORD, whose confidence is in him. He will be like a tree planted by the water that sends out its roots by the stream. It does not fear when heat comes; its leaves are always green. It has no worries in a year of drought and never fails to bear fruit" (Jer. 17:7-8).

That's "living land," wouldn't you say? That's God's goodness and faithfulness too. Aren't you grateful to know that your confidence rests in an unchanging God, a God whose character is not affected by the seasons?

MORE SCRIPTURE FOR STUDY:
2 Chronicles 7:1-3; Psalm 33:18-22;
Isaiah 32:17-18; James 1:17

Living Land

I am still confident of this: I will see the goodness of the LORD in the land of the living.

PSALM 27:13

OUR FARM IS A "living land" of horses, dogs, cats, chickens, fields, gardens, streams, and forests. That's not to mention the wild animals that make their homes on our land: turkeys, ducks, birds, coyote, deer, moose, bears, foxes— and those are just the ones I know about. A lot of life exists outside of my kitchen window.

I've given much thought over the years to what exactly is the "land of the living" that David speaks of. I've determined that the answer is really threefold.

First, the living land is God's created *earth*: "God saw all that he had made, and it was very good" (Gen. 1:31a). The first time that Genesis mentions "and God saw that it was good" is after He caused the land He created to separate from the water (1:10). Up to that point He had created light, sky, and water. Then He said that His created land was good.

Second, the living land is right where you *live*: "Dwell in the land and enjoy safe pasture" (Ps. 37:3). Safe pasture—your home—is His "Promised Land" to you of rest, security, and provision. That's regardless of whether your home is an apartment or a house, rented or owned. This land is holy ground because you have the Spirit of the living God within you.

Third, the living land is *you*—the fertile soil of your spirit: "You are God's field" (1 Cor. 3:9). If we are God's field, then the land of our souls is capable of growing and nurturing life—the life of Christ in us. Christ's goodness is reflected in how we live our lives.

Can you see why David wrote that God's goodness is in the land of the living? This is because God's created land is good, the holy ground of your home is good, and His Spirit dwells in you. Let's "taste and see that the LORD is good" (Ps. 34:8).

MORE SCRIPTURE FOR STUDY:
Exodus 31:13; Joshua 5:15; Proverbs 3:33;
Matthew 13:24-30, 36-43

The Lord Is All-Powerful

Great is your power ... all the earth bows down to you.

PSALM 66:3-4a

Multitasking

The LORD your God will bless you in all your harvest
and in all the work of your hands,
and your joy will be complete.

DEUTERONOMY 16:15b

I'M A CHECKLIST kind of person. A feeling of accomplishment boosts my ego when I can neatly check off my tasks for the day. I like the satisfaction of a met deadline.

Of course, there's a downside to being task-oriented. If jobs don't get done, a multitasker feels fragmented, defeated, and profitless.

I could look at the above verse from Deuteronomy and interpret it to mean that the Lord's blessing is dependent on accomplishment. I could read it to mean that the blessing comes in *how much* harvest is brought in or *how productive* is the work of my hands. But look at it more closely. This passage is part of the Feast of Tabernacles, which took place after the produce was gathered from the threshing floor. Everyone attended the feast: children, servants, widows, orphans, even out-of-towners. All were to give thanks for whatever had been harvested—much or little.

It's reassuring to know that the Lord is most interested in our best efforts and obedience, not the quantity of our work. Too often, multitaskers envision God with a giant checklist in hand, marking off our accomplishments and then determining our worthiness for blessings. Not so. The above verse says we're blessed in *all* of our harvest and *all* of the work of our hands. God is not so much interested in how much we've produced but rather in the heart effort of what we've produced. Do you see the difference?

If you're a multitasker like me, will you release the need to accomplish and instead trust the Lord to bless your best efforts, even if you can't check something off on a list? Pray with me:

Lord, thank You for creating me with an organized mind
that is goal-oriented. Please help me to set my goals on what and where
You want me to direct my efforts.

MORE SCRIPTURE FOR STUDY:
Psalm 86:11; Acts 20:24; Philippians 1:3-11;
Colossians 3:17, 23-24

Community Lost

In Christ we who are many form one body, and each member belongs to all the others.

ROMANS 12:5

THRIFTY NEW ENGLANDERS love to barter: vegetables given as payment for baby-sitting; wood exchanged for help with fencing; a field cleared as payment for a bulldozer. As a farmer—now as in the past—the service or produce you could provide was your form of currency. Traditionally, woodsheds were filled, meat stored in icehouses, hay cut and piled, and vegetables canned in rows—all through the exchange of services, produce, and talents.

This form of commerce nearly negated the need for actual money during the founding years of our country. A pervasive feeling of camaraderie and community undergirded the work ethic of the early colonial settlers. It was codependency in its best and truest form.

Now in typical urban America, we hardly know who our neighbors are, never mind their interests or talents. What happened?

We've lost the sense of needing one another for survival. Yet the Bible tells us to work together and care for each other. Repeatedly in the New Testament the church is referred to as the body of Christ. This body is made up of parts mutually joined for the same purpose: "so that there should be no division in the body, but that its parts should have equal concern for each other" (1 Cor. 12:25).

In the coming days, think of ways you can put into practice Paul's words of "equal concern." Does someone in your church need a friend with whom to talk? How about bringing a meal to an older person? Do you have a gift or talent you can share with someone? You can help bring a sense of community back into someone's life.

MORE SCRIPTURE FOR STUDY:
Psalm 133; Jeremiah 17:10; Matthew 10:42;
1 Corinthians 12:12-30

Self-Denied

*If anyone would come after me, he must deny himself and
take up his cross daily and follow me.*

LUKE 9:23

THE DAY STARTED as an Indian summer morning. My mother and I read-
ied our horses to go for a trail ride. Although a few clouds dotted the horizon,
we wanted to canter down the wood's trails for perhaps the last ride until spring.
After all, hunting season would soon arrive.

As we crunched our way through leaves and acorns, we didn't notice the
clouds creeping toward the sun until we found ourselves in the darkened
woods. We were still an hour from home when the sprinkling started. Shortly
afterward, a hard rain fell. In typical New England fashion a pocket of cold
air trailed along with the downpour.

The rain soaked through my windbreaker in less than five minutes. Torrents
ran down the backs of my calves into the depths of my boots. My gloves became
reservoirs at the fingertips. I began to shiver.

We arrived home in record time, our horses steaming from the dash. Our teeth chattered from the cold. As much as our desire was to get inside, dry off, and drink a cup of hot tea, we knew the horses needed tending to even more. We had to temporarily deny ourselves comfort to fulfill their needs.

I suddenly understood a glimpse of what it means to "deny [myself] and take up [my] cross." When we've been entrusted the care of something or someone, we're frequently required to release our own needs or desires. And does our selfishness ever show when we're challenged by someone else's needs!

I feel a strong conviction that if we put others first in our lives, as one aspect of our Christian witness, we might live in a less combative and neglected world. How about you? Have you felt challenged recently by the demands of others in your life? Can you take the Lord's words and apply them to your situation? Will you deny yourself and trust the Lord to give you the fulfillment of serving Him?

MORE SCRIPTURE FOR STUDY:
2 Chronicles 12:7-8; Romans 14:17-19;
Ephesians 4:29-5:2; Philippians 2:3-7

Take the Long View

Forgetting what is behind and straining toward what is ahead,
I press on toward the goal.

PHILIPPIANS 3:13-14

OUTSIDE OF OUR west-facing windows lies the six-mile ridge line of Mount Monadnock. In the spring the mountain seems to gather its muscles and rise to its full height. But in the fall, as its spring green changes into a patchwork of gray, it seems to recede in anticipation of the coming winter.

Each morning I drink my coffee at the kitchen table, watching the sun erase the last night shadows from the mountain's edges. On a good day I'll think about the diversity of the mountain—that it never seems to look the same two days in a row—and how I love the way it wears the different seasons. But on a grumpy day I'll just look at how dirty the kitchen window is. Then I'll get stuck there, never looking beyond the smudged glass.

The Lord showed me how I do this in other areas of my life. When I'm feeling optimistic, I have the long view—I have 20/20 vision about my future and feel excitement about it. But when I'm feeling pessimistic, my view is stunted. I can't look past my own situation.

How about you? Are you shortsighted or farsighted in your view of God's plan? Do you lose hope when you only see the smudged windows of your life? Or can you see God's faithfulness in the long run?

Proverbs 29:18 says, "Where there is no revelation, the people cast off restraint." If we don't have our eyes on the Lord, we become shortsighted. When we stop looking to God's glory and hope and instead see only dirty smudges, we lose our focus on the Lord.

We can choose to see past the smudges of day-to-day aggravations and instead concentrate on God's long-term plan. Will you look ahead with me to our hope in the Lord's future for us?

MORE SCRIPTURE FOR STUDY:
Proverbs 4:25; Isaiah 40:31;
Romans 8:18-25; 1 Corinthians 2:9;
2 Corinthians 10:7

God's Glory on Earth

The wild animals honor me, the jackals and the owls,
because I provide water in the desert and
streams in the wasteland.

ISAIAH 43:20

I JOKINGLY CALL MYSELF a daughter of Noah because I have a menagerie of pets. Yet being a caretaker of animals and their habitats is really no joke. Biblically speaking, animals had and still have a serious place in God's design. He created them before man and then created man to watch over them; He saved two of each kind on the ark and yet saved only eight people; unblemished animals were required as sacrifices until Jesus died for our sins; Jonah lived in the belly of a whale for three days to learn obedience; Jesus was born in a stable surrounded by animals; Jesus rode into Jerusalem on a young donkey and will ride a white horse when He returns to earth. Wouldn't you say that animals are pretty important to God's plan?

The above verse reminds us that animals recognize their dependency on

48

the God of nature. Doesn't it follow that we should recognize and care for nature—animals and the environment—too?

All of nature reflects God's sufficiency, provision, creativity, and faithfulness. God is faithful and present in everything, from the daily rising of the sun, to the yearly births of wild offspring, to the millions of species of plants, to the rain that waters all living things. What does the Bible say about God after He completed His six days of creation? "God saw all that he had made, and it was very good" (Gen. 1:31).

Think of ways you can honor the Lord by recognizing something in creation as a witness to His faithfulness. Birds flying in migration? Flowers you bought for your kitchen table? A huge rock, special tree, or wild animal near your home? Each time you find something in nature that reflects God's faithfulness, think on this verse: "The whole earth is full of his glory" (Isa. 6:3).

MORE SCRIPTURE FOR STUDY:
Genesis 1; Job 39; Psalm 19:1-6;
Psalm 136:4-9, 25-26

Holding On to Hope

The LORD gave and the LORD has taken away;
may the name of the LORD be praised.

JOB 1:21

EVEN AT AGE NINETY-FOUR and legally blind, my grandmother determinedly lives alone in her 200-year-old Cape Cod cottage. It's the house she and my grandfather shared until he died in 1992. Understandably she feels that leaving their home would mean abandoning my grandfather's memory. They invested their hearts in their house. Each creaky pine floorboard, aged beam, and uneven plastered wall holds a memory for her.

But they aren't all good memories. Tragedies followed her extended family over the years: the untimely death of her brother and his wife, leaving my grandparents four orphaned girls to raise; illnesses and accidents; two world wars and the great depression. People of her generation were shaped by hardships. They either fell into the abyss of self-pity or learned to be grateful for what was good.

My grandmother chose the second option. Even now in her whispery voice she'll say, "The Lord has been good to me…. The Lord is good." Has she forgotten those horrible times, the tear-drenched hours and weeks of coping? No, she hasn't forgotten. Instead she has chosen to take Job's words to heart: "The LORD gave and the LORD has taken away; may the name of the LORD be praised." She allowed the circumstances to shape her character and attitudes, while still holding on to the hope she invested in the Lord.

In our own circumstances we are offered the same choice. When you are feeling overwhelmed with circumstances, meditate on this passage: "We also rejoice in our sufferings, because we know that suffering produces perseverance; perseverance, character; and character hope. And hope does not disappoint us" (Rom. 5:3-5a).

MORE SCRIPTURE FOR STUDY:
Job 2:9-10; Psalm 100:5; Romans 8:37-39;
Philippians 4:8-9

Let It Rain

You heavens above, rain down righteousness;
let the clouds shower it down.

ISAIAH 45:8a

A COLD NOVEMBER RAIN chills the heart. Gray-brown tree branches scratch at the low gray clouds. All green seems lost. The post-vibrant colors and pre-holiday lull lays hold like a gray, soaking mist. During these "between weeks" until the snow falls, the landscape looks dreary. The soul feels cheerless until the joy of the holidays. The mind feels dull and thick. Even after just a short time of November rain, it seems absolutely impossible that there is a warm sun directly on the other side of the gray clouds.

Why does an April rain feel so refreshing, like a fulfilled promise of the Lord, while a November rain feels as though we've been abandoned? Because we can't see the result of a November rain as quickly as we see the result of a spring rain. A spring rain brings green immediately on its heels. A November rain brings more brown and gray with no promised green for six months.

Just because we don't have the instant gratification of green, does that mean we have been abandoned? Absolutely not! Continuing the above verse Isaiah says, "Let the earth open wide, let salvation spring up, let righteousness grow with it." Spring rains and fall rains both have to be received and absorbed before they are put to work. The fall rains just take longer.

This work of righteousness also applies to our souls. Are we ready to receive the showers of righteousness? Although a November rain in your spirit may be unpleasant for a time, know that through the showers the Lord is nurturing righteousness in you. Let it rain!

MORE SCRIPTURE FOR STUDY:
1 Samuel 26:21-25; Psalm 118:19-21;
Matthew 5:6; Romans 1:16-17

Say "Glory"

The voice of the LORD twists the oaks and strips the forest bare.
And in his temple all cry, "Glory!"

PSALM 29:9

OUTSIDE MY DAUGHTER'S BEDROOM window lived a giant oak that had been struck by lightning. A visible split went clear to its base. On windy days the two sides pulled away from each other. Daylight could be seen through the split. There was no doubt that the tree had to come down. It was dangerously close to our home. But I grieved the loss of its shade in the summer and the clatter of its branches in winter. It seemed a pity and a waste of God's creation.

Oak wood is the true "hardwood" of New England forests. It dulls a chain saw blade faster than other trees. Because it doesn't dent or scratch easily, oak wood is the wood of choice for flooring in homes.

An oak tree can live well beyond seventy-five years because of its solid base and tight infrastructure. The tree is nearly impossible to uproot in a storm. Yet the above verse says that God's *voice* "twists the oaks and strips the forest bare." That's a strong voice. That's one powerful God!

We may look at twisted or broken trees and think, *What a pity.* Or we may hear the groaning of trees tugged by the wind and feel afraid. But what does the above verse say about the response to God's voice twisting the oaks? "In his temple all cry, 'Glory!'" Why would we cry glory at the sight of broken trees or the threat of falling limbs? Because the power of the wind shows us a small glimpse of His awesome strength. Aren't you glad you're on His side? On the next windy day I'm going to yell, "Glory!"

MORE SCRIPTURE FOR STUDY:
*1 Chronicles 16:23-34; Psalm 97:1-6;
Isaiah 60:13; Revelation 19:6*

Freedom from Decay

Creation itself will be liberated from its bondage to decay
and brought into the glorious freedom
of the children of God.

ROMANS 8:21

THE SMELL OF ROTTING LEAVES and wood hangs in the cold November air. It's just a short time until the tangy smell will die out with the coming of snow. Until then the decaying leaves mulch into the ground, creating a spongy mat that seals in the moisture to feed the tree roots.

Even as the New England frost reaches depths of over three feet, the fall moisture is doing its work by nourishing the new growth below the frost line. The decay and rot from above is what feeds the tender roots below. Interesting concept, isn't it? Something good comes from the death of leaves and trees—a positive from a negative.

While Adam and Eve lived in the Garden of Eden, do you think any trees, animals, or plants there died? I don't believe there was death of any kind until after Adam and Eve sinned. Why? Because God's command was to "be fruitful and increase in number" (Gen. 1:28). This is a statement that encouraged an increase of life, not a decrease through death. There was only *creation* in Eden, not death.

But after sin, death took hold of man's soul and the land ("Cursed is the ground"—Genesis 3:17). The separation from God felt insurmountable. Thus entered God's promise of hope: His only Son Jesus.

Just as the decaying leaves nourish underground growth, we are reborn through Jesus' death and resurrection. This truth shows a positive from a negative: life from death. Because of His death we have the promise of eternal life. "It has now been revealed through the appearing of our Savior, Christ Jesus, who has destroyed death and has brought life and immortality to light through the gospel" (2 Tim. 1:10).

Take a walk this week and observe the signs of decay in nature. Aren't you glad your soul doesn't stay in a decaying state once you have accepted Jesus' eternal life?

MORE SCRIPTURE FOR STUDY:
Isaiah 53:12; Luke 24:36-49;
John 10:14-30; Romans 6:8-10

Glorious Freedom

*Creation itself will be liberated from its bondage to decay
and brought into the glorious freedom
of the children of God.*

ROMANS 8:21

LET'S FACE IT: our bodies are in a state of disrepair from the time we are born until we die. Backaches bother us, stress headaches plague us, colds and flu bugs run through our families. Our bodies are perpetually in "bondage to decay." Because of the consequences of original sin, we do not have perfect health, and we ultimately face certain physical death.

Most disconcerting are the life-threatening and life-altering diseases that, despite vast amounts of money being spent on research, have no cure and are increasing in incidence. I should know. My nine-year-old son has type I diabetes, meaning he is insulin-dependent. In 1997 he was one of the 13,000 new cases diagnosed each year in young people under twenty years old.

Any chronic disease takes a toll. The disease is costly to the wallet, to relationships, to time, to energy, and to one's faith. The latter is the most potentially harmful result.

It's easy to focus on the "problem" of the disease and not on the solution. David wrote, "But my eyes are fixed on you, O Sovereign LORD; in you I take refuge—do not give me over to death" (Ps. 141:8). His focus was on God, not on his own body.

God offers a promised hope in the "glorious freedom" of heaven, where there will no longer be suffering or sickness or decay. In the meantime "God has not deserted us in our bondage" (Ezra 9:9). "He has not despised or disdained the suffering of the afflicted one; he has not hidden his face from him but has listened to his cry for help" (Ps. 22:24).

Won't you pray with me for strength of character and preservation of dignity even as our bodies may decay? Our bodies may fade, but our spirits can remain intact as our hope is in God.

MORE SCRIPTURE FOR STUDY:
Exodus 23:20-26; Psalm 119:37-48;
Isaiah 30:18-21; 40:31

Thankful Freedom

Let us come before him with thanksgiving and extol him
with music and song.

PSALM 95:2

WHEN YOU THINK of Thanksgiving Day, what's the first thought that comes to your mind? Expressing thanks for blessings? Spending time with family? Gathering with friends to watch football? Perhaps for you Thanksgiving is all of the above, with delicious food at its center.

Our traditional Thanksgiving dinner, hosted by my sister, includes mashed potatoes, beans, squash, creamed onions, stuffing, pies, cranberry sauce, breads, gravy, and—of course—the turkey which had been raised on a local farm.

One Thanksgiving morning as Peter, the children, and I prepared to drive to my sister's house for family time and dinner, one of the children shouted that turkeys were strutting across our backyard. I laughed, certain they were trying to play a joke of "Made you look." But when I glanced out the kitchen window, there really *were* wild turkeys in the backyard! "Quick, get the gun!" I called, even though I knew that we have never owned a gun. That moment felt like a comedy, but later I reflected on the irony of the situation.

The Pilgrims instantly would have grabbed their guns, fired shots, laughed at their good fortune while plucking feathers, and then a few hours later said a heartfelt prayer of thanks as they sat down to eat roast turkey. That would have been a true Thanksgiving meal.

This Thanksgiving what aspects of the way our lives have changed since the time of the *Mayflower* Pilgrims inspire thanks in your heart? Certainly improved housing, a ready supply of food, family and friends, and health and longevity are some items for thanksgiving. The nearly 400 years' worth of hard-won quality of life improvements came at a huge cost to the first settlers on New England soil. Let's remember this Thanksgiving to give thanks for the most basic of our Christian rights: the freedom to give thanks.

MORE SCRIPTURE FOR STUDY:
Psalms 30:11-12; 75:1; Mark 14:22-26;
2 Corinthians 9:6-15

Keep the Fire Burning

The fire must be kept burning on the altar continuously;
it must not go out.

LEVITICUS 6:13

NEW ENGLANDERS SAY that wood is the fuel that warms you twice. The first time is when you cut, chop, and stack it. (Depending on how you pile your wood, that could be three separate warming sessions!) The second time is when you burn it.

On cold late fall mornings, houses in New England valleys puff smoke from their chimneys. The smoke creeps across the lowlands, insulating the town from the cold world. Some homes exclusively burn wood for all of their heating needs while others use a combination of wood and oil. Either way, the labored-for wood is consumed in a quick blaze, giving a blast of heat, and then leaving just ashes.

The book of Leviticus describes how priests were instructed to keep the fire burning on the altar. "The fire must be kept burning on the altar continuously; it must not go out" (Lev. 6:13). Having used wood-burning stoves in our home in the past, I know how difficult that command is! A person needs to tend the hearth nearly constantly to keep the fire burning.

Do you see the parallel between the instructions to the Israelites and to us? The Lord doesn't want our inner fire to die either. Why? An extinguished fire is hard to rekindle. The colder the ashes, the more energy, resources, and time it requires to rekindle the flame.

How can we keep our inner fires burning? The Holy Spirit in us keeps our faith kindled. "He will baptize you with the Holy Spirit and with fire" (Matt. 3:11). We have a job to do too. To keep your fire burning, add more fuel every day in the form of time alone with your heavenly Father.

MORE SCRIPTURE FOR STUDY:
Deuteronomy 4:23-24; 1 Kings 18:36-39;
2 Corinthians 1:18-22;
1 Thessalonians 5:16-24

The Lord Is Listening

Does he who implanted the ear not hear?

PSALM 94:9a

God's Whole Picture

Then we shall see face to face. Now I know in part; then
I shall know fully, even as I am fully known.

1 CORINTHIANS 13:12

I HAD BEEN ASKING THE LORD—a little impatiently I might add—for a revelation about a certain situation. I wanted to know the full outcome, but He had only given me a little piece of information.

Walking to the barn one night to give my horses a late night snack, I saw the moon resting low in the sky, as if pausing before slipping over the horizon. Part of the moon was lit; the rest lay in shadow. The moon was in its waxing stage, awaiting the inevitable tilt and turn on its axis to bring the whole sphere out of the earth's shadow and back into the sunlight's path.

Looking at the moon, I was reminded that just as we can only see part of the moon during certain times of the month, we can only know "in part" what God's plan is at any given time. The rest has yet to be illuminated. He doesn't reveal the whole picture to us for a number of reasons. Maybe He wants to keep us tethered to His side in faith. Maybe we have something to learn while we wait. Maybe the whole picture would be too much for us to understand.

We may perceive the vague outline of the bigger, fuller plan now while we wait. We may not see the "full moon" of His plan for years, or it may be wholly plain tomorrow.

Faith grows as more and more "Sonlight" falls on your situation. This week, think about what you know "in part" and in what ways God will help you grow until you know "in full." Will you keep watch in faith, knowing that the complete plan is there, yet not fully illuminated?

MORE SCRIPTURE FOR STUDY:
Jeremiah 29:11; Romans 5:1-2;
2 Corinthians 5:7; Hebrews 11:1-3

The Eternal Word

The grass withers and the flowers fall, but the word
of our God stands forever.

ISAIAH 40:8

CRUNCHING THROUGH a frozen field, I was reminded again of the temporary nature of all of life. The last vestiges of fall are long gone. The brown grass feels brittle underfoot from frost.

The saying goes that every person in the world will assuredly experience two things: birth and death. It's true in nature too. Trees are struck by lightning in the summer and crash to the ground and rot. Most household pets have a life expectancy of less than fifteen years. Annual plants are short-lived, lasting only through the warm seasons.

So why are we affronted when something dies? After all, death is expected. I believe the dismay comes because we can't grasp the concept of eternity. Eternity is not temporary. Yet all we have experienced to date is temporary. So how can we understand eternity? We live in the here and now, suspended between the beauty and perfection of creation in Eden and our final home of eternity in heaven.

Ecclesiastes 3:11 says, "He has ... set eternity in the hearts of men; yet they cannot fathom what God has done from beginning to end." We have "eternity" in our hearts if we have accepted Christ's gift of salvation, thereby granting us entrance into heaven. That gift is eternal. But just as King Solomon says in the verse from Ecclesiastes, even with that assurance, we still can't know all there is to know about God's eternal purposes. Only God has that knowledge.

This is what the above verse from Isaiah communicates to me. The Word of the Lord stands forever. Though grasping the forever of eternity is hard, we can trust that God's Word is eternal even when we can only see what is temporary.

MORE SCRIPTURE FOR STUDY:
2 Samuel 22:31; Psalm 119:89-96;
Daniel 4:1-3; 1 Timothy 1:15-17

White Days

He says to the snow, "Fall on the earth."

JOB 37:6a

I LOOK FORWARD to the coming of snow in New England. Snow covers the brown stains of earth. I love the way the fields and woods wear the snow, as if they've put on new clothes for the season.

Snow is an excuse for what I call a "white day"—not just literally white outside, but white inside. Enough snow cancels school, work, plans, and appointments. It makes for a free day—a white day when everything can be erased from the calendar. Time slows and the day stretches ahead as the most important duties become an invitation to go skiing across the pasture, make snowmen with the children, or drink a cup of tea and read.

You don't have to be snowbound to experience white days. How about a day when you feel mildly ill or when you have a sudden cancellation?

A white day is a gift. It's like a day of rest in the middle of the week. But your to-do list can act as a stubborn reminder of what you *can't* do on a white day. Consider God's plan though. "Many are the plans in a man's heart, but it is the LORD's purpose that prevails" (Prov. 19:21).

What is His purpose for you on white days? Can you accept a white day with a spirit of thanksgiving? Can you release your plans for the day and let the Holy Spirit direct you in how to spend your hours? Maybe you could write notes of encouragement to friends, call relatives and catch up on news, or spend hours praying. Make a plan now for when you might be granted a white day. As you plan, look forward to how the Lord will minister to you.

MORE SCRIPTURE FOR STUDY:
Psalm 46:10; 19; Acts 3:19;
2 Corinthians 13:14

Certain Hope

Long ago I learned from your statutes that you establish them to last forever.

PSALM 119:152

A COUPLE OF WEEKS before Christmas on a Saturday afternoon, the children, the dogs, Peter, and I pile in the car and drive to a Christmas tree farm. We stroll up and down the rows until we find "the one." The requirements are that the tree must not be too wide on the bottom; it must be thick with one straight branch at the top for the angel. The tree must also have a flatter side to tuck against the wall. After finding "the one," we knock the snow off. Peter kneels and saws the stump. Back at home, Christmas music and hot chocolate accompany the decorating.

Why do we like to bring a tree into the house for Christmas? Other than tradition, I love to have green inside when the outside world looks so bleak. I love the sharp pine or spruce smell. It's clean and fresh, as if I've opened all the windows for new air.

I like to think that the Lord created pine trees to have something that is always green. That's why they are called *evergreens*—they are forever green. Green is a sign of life and constant hope, particularly for those who live in places with clearly differing seasons. Even in the midst of a blizzard or rain, the green is always visible. Don't you find great comfort in that?

Isaiah 55:13 reflects God's intention that the pine tree offer hope. "Instead of the thornbush will grow the pine tree, and instead of briers the myrtle will grow. This will be for the LORD's renown, for an everlasting sign, which will not be destroyed."

If you bring an evergreen into your home this year or observe them growing, will you reflect on Isaiah's words that the always-green pine tree represents a portion of God's everlasting promises to us?

MORE SCRIPTURE FOR STUDY:
Psalms 92:1-2; 130:5-7; Micah 7:1-7;
Hebrews 10:23; 11:1-3

Cumulative Effect

As the rain and snow come down from heaven, and do not return
to it without watering the earth ... so is my word
that goes out from my mouth: it will not return to me empty,
but will accomplish what I desire and achieve the purpose
for which I sent it.

ISAIAH 55:10-11

A SNOWDRIFT IS CREATED one snowflake at a time. One snowflake by itself is insignificant, barely perceptible. A snowflake won't last by itself. It disappears as soon as it hits the ground if more don't follow shortly. It takes literally trillions and trillions of flakes to create a winter scene.

I've heard that each snowflake actually starts in the upper atmosphere as a tiny piece of grit or dust. As gravity pulls it toward the earth, moisture covers it and then freezes. More moisture spiders out from it. Behold—a snowflake is born, each one uniquely different from all the others.

Snowflakes combine to form drifts, cover fields, and blanket trees and bushes. The collective effect is a radiant white enveloping the drab browns and grays of winter. One might even say that one of the reasons for snow is to give us the perfect illustration of Christ's taking our dirty sins and washing them into whiteness (see Psalm 51:7).

But there's another illustrative reason suggested in the above verse from Isaiah. It reminds us that the snow (and rains) have a very definite purpose: to water God's creation. Likewise, God tells us that His word has a desired outcome. His Word will fulfill His purpose: "watering" and nurturing His people.

With Christians as with snowflakes, it sometimes takes many to have an effect. We can't leave ministering, witnessing, or evangelizing to more "qualified" people. You are qualified because of your uniqueness. Each of us is needed to fulfill God's plan. What is this plan? Jesus' own words describe it: "Therefore go and make disciples of all nations, baptizing them in the name of the Father and of the Son and of the Holy Spirit.... And surely I am with you always, to the very end of the age" (Matt. 28:19-20).

I'm willing to be part of the "snowdrift effect" by connecting with other Christians to reach "all nations." Are you?

MORE SCRIPTURE FOR STUDY:
Esther 4:12-17; Mark 16:15;
2 Timothy 4:1-5; 2 Peter 1:3-11

The Good Way

Stand at the crossroads and look; ask for the ancient paths,
ask where the good way is, and walk in it,
and you will find rest for your souls.

JEREMIAH 6:16a

I STRAPPED SNOWSHOES over my warm boots and eagerly set out across the yard. I padded toward the road that twists and turns through several miles of wooded property adjacent to our farm and leads to a stream that never freezes.

The wide trail, edged on either side by snow-covered stone walls, was once used as a main thoroughfare with other stone-wall-lined roads leading off on either side. I wondered how many sheep, cattle, and horses had followed this same route, moving from one part of town to another. They followed the road in the spring to feed on lush pastures through the summer and then returned by the same route in the fall to their winter homes.

Nearing the brook, I saw the remnants of old fence posts and the half-buried steel rim of a wagon wheel pushing up through the snow. I wondered about the history of all these ancient roads on which I've skied or ridden. I knew that what is now overgrown and reclaimed by the forest once served a purpose as either pastureland or roads. There was no way a person could lose his or her way traveling between the stone boundary walls. The path was clearly defined. These were the "good ways": time tested, clear, safe, and efficient.

There's security in the "good ways" God has set before us too. Isaiah 30:21 describes God's direction: "Your ears will hear a voice behind you, saying, 'This is the way; walk in it.'" But do we *know* the "good ways" of our Creator? Hosea cautions, "My people are destroyed from a lack of knowledge" (4:6). Do we live by His commandments and promises, which affect not only us but our relationships with others?

His ancient ways, from His first inscription of the commandments to now, form the path we can follow today. Like the stone-wall-lined roads, the route is clearly laid out. It's our choice whether or not we'll stay on track.

MORE SCRIPTURE FOR STUDY:
Deuteronomy 7:9-16;
Psalms 103:17-18; 119:25-32;
1 Peter 2:21

House Building

Heaven is my throne, and the earth is my footstool.
Where is the house you will build for me?

ISAIAH 66:1a

IMAGINE THIS: God is so immense and pervasive that the earth is but a place to rest His feet. Compared to the vast extent of heaven, we reside on just a small area. It makes you feel pretty minuscule, doesn't it? This is the sentiment of David's words: "What is man that you are mindful of him?" (Ps. 8:4).

As David concluded, God not only is mindful of us (the proof being His intimate involvement in our lives), but He also created everything we see around us as a reminder of His creativity and His glory.

Yet God's question in the verse above reminds us that all of God cannot be "contained" in a human-built place, no matter how grand. But do you sense a deeper question in God's words? I do. Where, ultimately, does the Lord want us to "build a house" for Him? In our hearts. Our hearts are His temple, as 1 Corinthians 3:16 explains. "Don't you know that you yourselves are God's temple and that God's Spirit lives in you?" Building a temple of worship to the Lord in our hearts reminds us that we have a responsibility as part of His creation to provide a place for His glory to be proclaimed: through our lives.

We can't build a huge external place to house our Lord, but we certainly can build an internal one for His Spirit. I want my inner house for Him to be filled with praise for His creation. How about you?

MORE SCRIPTURE FOR STUDY:
2 Chronicles 6:36—7:3; Proverbs 24:3-4;
1 Corinthians 3:10-17; 2 Corinthians 6:16

Creating Time

*The sun stopped in the middle of the sky and
delayed going down about a full day.
There has never been a day like it before or since.*

JOSHUA 10:13b-14a

THE WINTER SOLSTICE, shorter by just a minute or two than all the other days of the year, accentuates my feeling of losing time every day. As December ticks on toward the solstice on the twenty-first, the light coming through my living room windows changes. It's softer and there's less of it. It's not my imagination that the days get shorter before Christmas—they really do! The countdown to the solstice compounds my frantic efforts to get everything that requires sunlight done during the daylight hours. In my mind I squeal:

Stop the clock!
Delay the sun!
Multiply my time!
It seems that the less sun there is, the more I need to do!
Of course the Lord doesn't stop the clock for me, as the above Scripture

describes. He's only done that once, and for a very good reason: so the Israelites could win a war.

No, my crisis of time has nothing to do with a war. But I have noticed one thing the Lord does for me when I issue a sincere cry for more time: He helps me multiply my time. He shows me how to make up for lost time. He may give me a flash of understanding as to how to order my priorities for the day. He also may help me decide where my focus needs to be. When I yield to Him, I find that my day runs more efficiently. But there is a caveat. It's only when I invest time in Him that He'll invest time in me. It's that simple.

Don't let the hectic pace of pre-Christmas and diminishing daylight allow you to lose time. Force yourself to make time for the Lord each day this week. Trust Him to multiply time for you.

MORE SCRIPTURE FOR STUDY:
Psalm 31:15; Hosea 10:12; Luke 11:3;
2 Corinthians 6:2; 2 Peter 3:8

Making Room

There was no room for them in the inn.

LUKE 2:7

THERE WERE NO SPECIAL PREPARATIONS, no messenger sent ahead to scout out a bed. Mary and Joseph found that there simply was no room. Were they delayed in arriving because the going was slow with Mary? Others of the lineage of David had already claimed all the beds in Bethlehem. This was Joseph's very own extended family. Yet there was still no room! Maybe he knocked on other doors; maybe he pleaded; maybe he pointed a finger at Mary's belly. Heads shook no. The words "no room" hung in the evening air.

Finally a solution was presented. "A stable? Where?" At a quick nod from Mary, Joseph probably replied, "We'll go there." Tired, but grateful, they turned away from the packed inn.

The Bethlehem inn, like any inn, was likely the center of the village where money exchanged hands in commerce; where the townspeople met to gossip; where a person could eat, drink, and rest. But Joseph and Mary did not take part in the goings-on in town that day. Jesus arrived as He would leave— set apart.

Just as He was set apart from mankind in His life and perfection, He was set apart from the inn in Bethlehem. What does the "inn" represent for people in the twenty-first century? Hearts. For people who haven't asked Him into their hearts, He is still set apart. There's still "no room." They've left Him in the stable.

Revelation 3:20 says, "Here I am! I stand at the door and knock. If anyone hears my voice and opens the door, I will come in and eat with him, and he with me." That's inviting Him in, isn't it? That's opening the welcome door wide and saying, "Leave the stable and come into my heart."

Here's our challenge: This Christmas explain to an unbeliever what "no room" means in our "me-first" culture. With self-centeredness comes no room for Jesus. Let's help people open the door to their hearts, making room for the Lord Jesus. No more "no room."

MORE SCRIPTURE FOR STUDY:
Matthew 22:1-14; 28:18-20; Luke 2:1-20; John 8:34-38; 1 Peter 3:15

Humble Beginnings

She gave birth to her firstborn, a son. She wrapped him in cloths
and placed him in a manger.

LUKE 2:7

WHEN JESUS WAS BORN, I doubt that the owner of the stable had recently cleaned all the refuse out of the stalls. He surely didn't know someone was going to stay in the barn, never mind give birth in it.

The stable where Jesus was born was not quaint and was certainly not clean-smelling. It likely had a strong ammonia smell since the buildup of animal waste melds into a pungent gas. Also, most animals aren't very particular about where they relieve themselves. The stuff no doubt covered much of the dirt floor.

So why did God, who has control over every situation, not provide at least a simple bed for Mary in a home or the inn? How could He allow His only Son to be born in such a place? Because right from the start Jesus was humble. His parents were humble, submissive, and obedient. The Bible doesn't say that they complained at the injustice. They seemed to accept it as part of God's plan.

I can also imagine Mary wrapping her baby in tight clothes, as tradition dictated, but also to protect Him from the prickly hay in the manger. I wonder if when He wore a crown of thorns some thirty-odd years later, she remembered the swaddling clothes and wished she could do the same again to protect Him from the thorns piercing His head. But again she must have to come to accept the crown and the inhumane injustice as part of God's plan for Jesus.

Paul challenges us to become more Christlike in our Christian faith (see Philippians 1:21). Yet in humility could any of us do what Mary and Joseph did? Even though I own a barn and am accustomed to its smells, I can't imagine giving birth in one. If the Lord called me to that level of humility and obedience, would I resist or trust Him like Mary, despite what I believed to be an injustice?

Will you join with me this Christmas and think about the humility with which our Lord entered the world? How can we emulate His humility in our Christian walks?

MORE SCRIPTURE FOR STUDY:
Isaiah 66:2; Matthew 11:29;
Philippians 2:5-8; Titus 3:1-11;
Hebrews 2:14

Joy Burst

Shout for joy to the LORD, all the earth, burst into jubilant song
with music.... Shout for joy before the LORD, the King.

PSALM 98:4-6b

PARTRIDGES (the ones that live in pear trees at Christmas) are plump, camouflage-brown birds. In the New England winter woods they burrow under the snow or allow a snowstorm to bury them. The snow hides them, insulating them against the cold and predators. Then, either from a disturbance, hunger, or simply enough rest, they burst out into the daylight in a mini-explosion of feathers and powdery snow. They flit off to snack or perch, eyeing the white world around them.

Sometimes a hole in the snow—a scattering of drift clumps—can be found where a partridge had rested quietly, then spooked out in a glory burst of brown-winged strength, up into the open air and freedom.

Have you ever felt a bursting of joy in your spirit? I can imagine how the partridge feels. I have a sudden instinct to lift my arms heavenward in a display of happiness and freedom. My joy bursts come from a touch from the Lord on my heart. He knows what ministers to my spirit. He puts things in my life that spark joy: watching my daughter ride her horse, the look of delight on my son's face when he's snowboarding, listening to my husband read a story to our children, or a soul-connection with a friend.

Will you trust the Lord each day to give you a taste of joy? Joy isn't dependent on an event or circumstance. I know that the Lord wants all of His children to experience joy in all He has created. Sometimes, however, like the partridge, we have to stretch our wings outside the comfortable shelter of our own environment to see and feel joy. Will you look for joy in and beyond your surroundings today? Will you stretch your arms heavenward to the Lord as a gesture of joy?

MORE SCRIPTURE FOR STUDY:
Psalms 4:6-7; 100; Isaiah 55:12;
1 Peter 1:8-9

This Is My Father's World

This is my Father's world,
And to my listening ears
All nature sings, and round me rings
The music of the spheres.
This is my Father's world,
I rest me in the thought
Of rocks and trees, of skies and seas—
His hand the wonders wrought.

This is my Father's world,
The birds their carols raise;
The morning light, the lily white
Declare their Maker's praise.
This is my Father's world,
He shines in all that's fair;
In the rustling grass I hear Him pass,
He speaks to me everywhere.

This is my Father's world,
O let me ne'er forget
That though the wrong seems oft so strong,
God is the Ruler yet.
This is my Father's world,
The battle is not done;
Jesus who died, shall be satisfied,
And earth and heav'n be one.

MALTBIE D. BABCOCK

A NATIVE NEW ENGLANDER, Elizabeth Hoekstra lives on a farm in southern New Hampshire with her husband, Peter, and their two children. She holds an R.N. degree, with a concentration in psychology and maternal health, and has worked in both hospital and community health settings. Currently she manages Direct Path Ministries, which encourages women and families to form deeper interpersonal relationships under the lordship of Jesus Christ. Elizabeth also gardens, shows her horse Galilee, and enjoys skiing, boating, kayaking, biking, and hiking with her family.

Other Crossway books by Elizabeth M. Hoekstra

Keeping Your Family Close When Frequent Travel Pulls You Apart

Just for Girls

Just for Moms

A Season of Rejoicing

A Season of Gladness

A Season of Stillness

With Mary Bradford
Chronic Kids, Constant Hope

MARLENE M^cLOUGHLIN WAS BORN IN BUFFALO, NEW YORK, and grew up in southern California. She received a degree in art history from Barnard College in New York City and a degree in drawing "with high distinction" from California College of Arts and Crafts.

In 1998 she went to Rome to work on her book *Road to Rome* (Chronicle Books) and decided to stay because of the beauty of the landscape and because dogs are allowed almost everywhere. She lives with Kiddo, a tortoise shell cat, and Barely, a German-Italian shepherd mix ... both pets are bilingual!

Marlene works from home on projects that vary from logo design to wall paintings. Her internationally award-winning books include: *Diane Seed's Rome for All Seasons, Across the Aegean,* and *The Passionate Observer.* Her clients include Linda Ronstadt, Williams-Sonoma, Ten Speed Press, and HarperCollins.

The typeface for this book is Adobe Garamond, originally designed by Claude Garamond in 1532. His oldstyle designs, based on the Aldine model, were the typefaces of choice in the composing rooms of printers well into the 18th century. In 1989 Robert Slimbach modified the design of this typeface slightly for Adobe, and it remains a favorite for book designers today.

The script used throughout is Escrita, a three weight, hand-drawn face designed by Mário Feliciano for T-26 in 1997.

The interior for this series was set by Joe Rosewell and Rose Graham.